dway
COUNCIL

i

Th‾
Not-A-Troll

'The Not-A-Troll'
An original concept by Kate Poels
© Kate Poels 2022

Illustrated by Marina Pérez Luque

Published by MAVERICK ARTS PUBLISHING LTD
Studio 11, City Business Centre, 6 Brighton Road,
Horsham, West Sussex, RH13 5BB
© Maverick Arts Publishing Limited August 2022
+44 (0)1403 256941

A CIP catalogue record for this book is available at the British Library.

ISBN 978-1-84886-903-5

www.maverickbooks.co.uk

This book is rated as: Turquoise Band (Guided Reading)

The Not-A-Troll

By Kate Poels

Illustrated by
Marina Pérez Luque

Henry lived in a house with a big garden.

At the end of the garden was a little stream.

One hot day, Henry went down to the little stream to cool off his toes. He was splashing his feet in the water when he saw two eyes peeping out of the weeds.

"Hello," Henry called.

The eyes blinked.

"Do you want to come and play?" Henry asked. Then...

...out came a troll.

Henry could tell it was a troll because he had seen lots of trolls in books.

He was worried because he knew trolls were not fun to play with.

"Wow," said Henry. "I've never met a troll before."

The troll looked surprised.

"I'm not a troll, I'm a not-a-troll," he said.

"Oh!" said Henry. He wondered what a not-a-troll was, but he thought it was rude to ask.

"I'm Henry," he said. "What's your name?"

"I'm Bobbo."

Henry and Bobbo played by the stream. They threw pebbles and looked for newts. Bobbo was very good at both of these things. He was also very funny.

Henry was surprised at how much fun a not-a-troll was to play with.

"I have to go home now," said Henry. "Would you like to come with me?"

"Yes please," said Bobbo. "I would really like that."

They walked up the garden path to where Henry's little sister, Izzy, was playing with her teddy.

Izzy could tell Henry's new friend was a troll because he smelled of pond weed. She also knew that trolls are not kind. She was a bit scared, so she gave Ted a big hug, just to keep him safe.

"Hello," said Bobbo. "Are you okay?"

"I've never met a troll before," said Izzy.

"I'm not a troll, I'm a not-a-troll," said Bobbo.

"Oh!" said Izzy. "Hello, I'm Izzy."

"I'm Bobbo."

Izzy was happy when Bobbo showed

her how to make a seat for Ted out of

pebbles.

He also showed them both how to make little stick insects with some of the tall grass. Izzy liked the not-a-troll and was happy he had come to play.

"Dinner's ready," called Mum.

Henry, Izzy and Bobbo went inside.

"Can our new friend stay for dinner?"
Henry asked.

"Yes," said Mum. "But you must all
wash your hands first."

Mum knew there was a troll in her house
because of the mess on the floor. She'd
heard that trolls were rude and dirty
and was very surprised to see one in the
kitchen.

"I've never met a troll before," she said.

"I'm not a troll, I'm a not-a-troll," said Bobbo.

"Oh!" said Mum. "I'm so sorry."

"His name is Bobbo," said Henry.

Mum got another plate out and dished up some pie for Bobbo.

The not-a-troll ate all his food and helped to clear the plates away afterwards.

"Thank you very much for the yummy food," said Bobbo. "That was the best pie I have ever had."

Mum looked at the not-a-troll in surprise.

It was nice to have such a good guest in

the house.

"You're welcome," she smiled.

After dinner, Henry and Izzy showed Bobbo their toy box. They played with the ball. Then they played a game of cards. They made a tower with blocks, and they made a tent from a sheet. The not-a-troll was good fun and very helpful.

Izzy's tower fell down, but Bobbo helped her to build a stronger one. Henry's tent would not stay up, so Bobbo helped him make that strong too.

Mum gave them all milk and cookies to eat in the tent. The not-a-troll was the first one to say, 'thank you'.

When it was time for him to go, Bobbo

made sure he helped tidy away the

tent, the ball, the cards and the blocks.

"I've had a really brilliant time," Bobbo said.

"I've never met a family of *giants* before!"

Henry and Izzy looked at each other and then back at the not-a-troll.

"But we're *not* giants," they said.

"Oh," said Bobbo. He wondered what Henry and his family were, but he thought it was rude to ask.

He smiled and waved goodbye to Henry, Izzy and their mum. Then the not-a-troll went back down to the end of the garden...

...to tell his family all about the **not-a-giant**

he had met by the stream!

Quiz

1. Where did Henry first meet the not-a-troll?
a) At the park
b) By the stream
c) On the beach

2. What is the name of the not-a-troll?
a) Bibbo
b) Bob
c) Bobbo

3. What is Henry's little sister called?
a) Lizzy
b) Izzy
c) Lucy

4. What did the not-a-troll teach Henry and his sister how to make?
a) Grass stick insects
b) Paper aeroplanes
c) A tree house

5. What did the not-a-troll think Henry and his family were?
a) Humans
b) Trolls
c) Giants

Turn over for answers

Book Bands for Guided Reading

The Institute of Education book banding system is a scale of colours that reflects the various levels of reading difficulty. The bands are assigned by taking into account the content, the language style, the layout and phonics. Word, phrase and sentence level work is also taken into consideration.

Maverick Early Readers are a bright, attractive range of books covering the pink to white bands. All of these books have been book banded for guided reading to the industry standard and edited by a leading educational consultant.

Pink
Red
Yellow
Blue
Green
Orange
Turquoise
Purple
Gold
White

To view the whole Maverick Readers scheme, visit our website at www.maverickearlyreaders.com

Or scan the QR code above to view our scheme instantly!

Quiz Answers: 1b, 2c, 3b, 4a, 5c